Teaching Little Fingers to Play More Blues and Boogie

Piano Solos With Optional Teacher Accompaniments
By
Carolyn Miller

CONTENTS

12604

Play It!
Optional Teacher Accompaniment

Carolyn Miller

Moderately fast

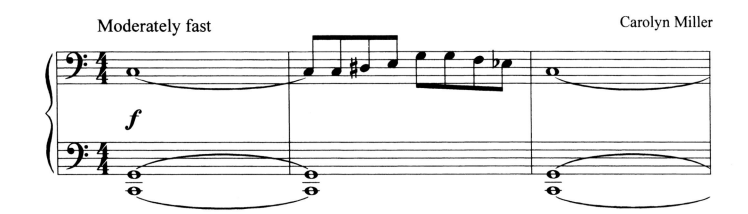

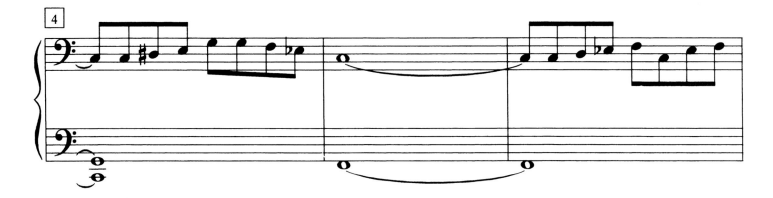

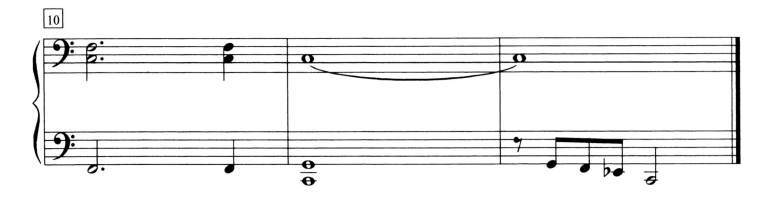

Play It!

Play both hands one octave higher when performing as a duet.

Carolyn Miller

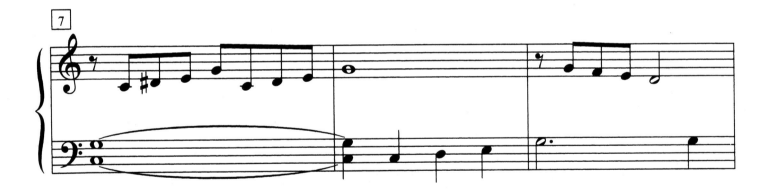

When playing as a duet,
play this note with the
L.H.

Got the Beat!

Optional Teacher Accompaniment

Carolyn Miller

Got the Beat!

Play both hands one octave higher when performing as a duet.

Moderato

Carolyn Miller

12604

Got the Blues!
Optional Teacher Accompaniment

Carolyn Miller

Got the Blues!

Play both hands one octave higher when performing as a duet.

Carolyn Miller

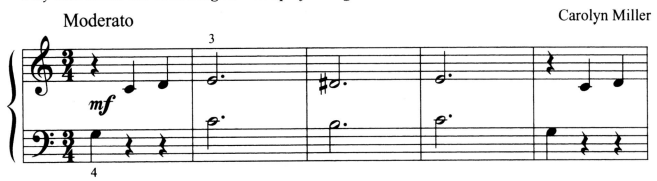

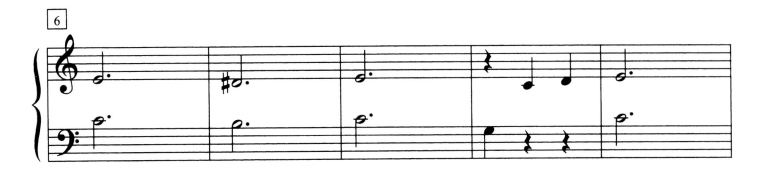

Optional Teacher Accompaniment

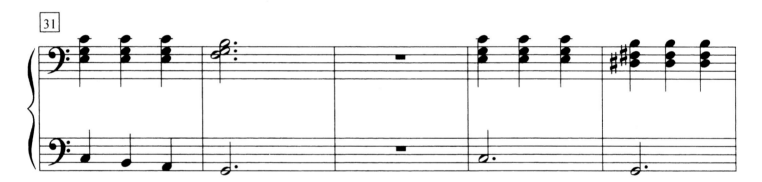

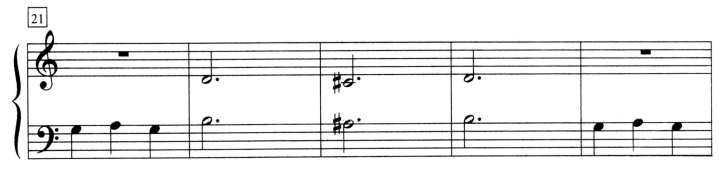

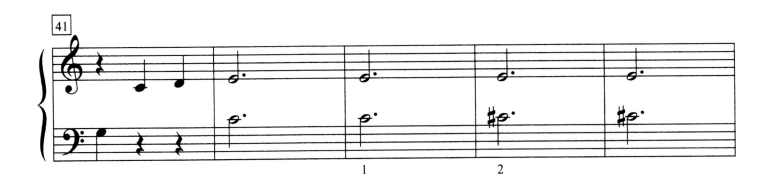

Optional Teacher Accompaniment

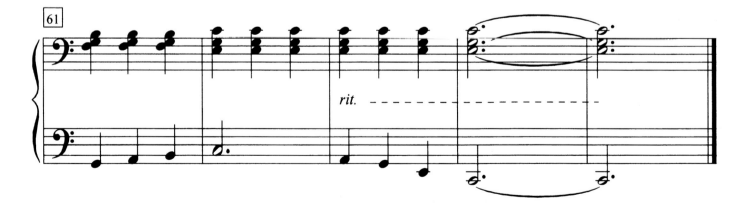

11

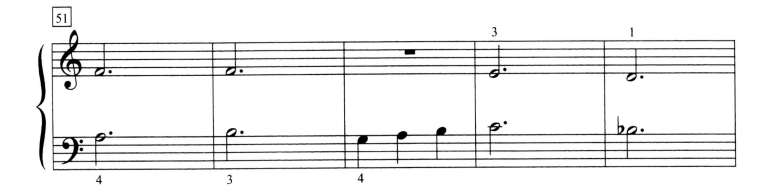

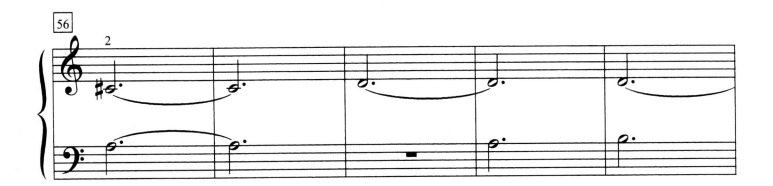

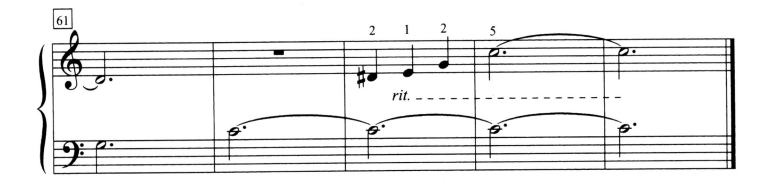

The Muffin Man
Optional Teacher Accompaniment

Carolyn Miller

The Muffin Man

Carolyn Miller

12604

Boogie Bass
Optional Teacher Accompaniment

Swing

Carolyn Miller

With energy

Boogie Bass

Swing

Play both hands one octave higher when performing as a duet.

With energy

Carolyn Miller

When the Saints Go Marching In
Optional Teacher Accompaniment

Carolyn Miller

With energy

When the Saints Go Marching In

Play both hands one octave higher when performing as a duet.

Carolyn Miller

With energy

Old MacDonald Had a Farm

Teacher Accompaniment

Carolyn Miller

12604

Old MacDonald Had a Farm

Swing

Play both hands one octave higher when performing as a duet.

Happily

Carolyn Miller

John Jacob Jingleheimer Schmidt
Optional Teacher Accompaniment

Carolyn Miller

With energy

John Jacob Jingleheimer Schmidt

Play both hands one octave higher when performing as a duet.

Carolyn Miller

The Spider Song
Optional Teacher Accompaniment

Carolyn Miller

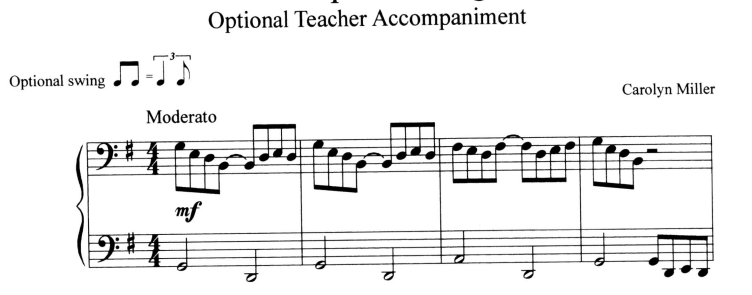

The Spider Song

Optional swing

Play both hands one octave higher when performing as a duet.

Moderato

Carolyn Miller